Chapter One

The Beginning of the War

The War of 1812 doesn't begin in 1812, or even in the 1800s.

The end of the 18th century was a politically troubled time. The era that began with the Seven Years War in 1755 wouldn't begin to culminate until the century turned, and wouldn't come to a close until 1815, when the War of 1812 finally ended.

With the might of the English, French and Spanish navies, conflicts became more global as further battlefields came within reach. The Seven Years war, also called The French and Indian Wars in America, The War of Conquest in Canada, The Pomeranian War in Sweden, the Third Carnatic War on the Indian sub-continent, and the Third Silesian war in Austria, was the first truly global war, and many consider it to be a precursor to World War One.

The war began on the American continent when Britain attacked French positions and seized hundreds of French merchant ships in the disputed territories of New France. Prussia then invaded Saxony, pulling in their English and Austrian allies into the conflict. Many of the middle and smaller powers attempted to stay clear of war, and by the time of the Treaty of Paris and the Treaty of Hubertusburg, which effectively ended the war in 1763, the balance of power in Europe had shifted significantly.

Great Britain came through the war gaining large territories in North America, the West Indies, and the West African coast, and regulated trade in India. France found itself saddled with a heavy war debt, and lost most of her colonies.

Right on the heels of that conflict the American Revolution proved something unprecedented — that a remote colony could overthrow a superpower and declare itself its own sovereign state. Even more drastic was that the colony, now an independent country, had no monarchy. A freely-elected political system had overthrown a monarchy rooted in centuries of tradition.

Burdened with the heavy debt of war, the people of France entered a time of economic depression and hardship. There were many complicated reasons for the French Revolution of 1792, but the excesses of the aristocracy and the clergy while the country was experiencing bad harvests and crushing debts lay heavily on the general populace. This led to a feeling of unrest, and ultimately revolt.

The traditional position of the Roman-Catholic church was absolute monarchy by divine decree, meaning the king has absolute power by the will of God, and that God gives a country the king it needs or deserves. At the end of the 18th century, this idea was being replaced by the Age of Enlightenment which used reason, scientific rigor, and reductionism – examining the differences in philosophical positions and reducing them into simpler statements.

In January 1793, King Louis XVI was publicly executed, sending a shockwave through the European aristocracy. A monarch's people had risen up and killed their "rightful" king. Without a king, France had now become a threat to monarchies across Europe and found themselves vulnerable. The pro-tem government who called themselves The Committee of Public Safety established the famous Reign of Terror from 1793-1974 where over 16,000 people were executed by the guillotine.

The Committee of Public Safety was accused of corruption and collapsed in a coup led by Napoleon Bonaparte in 1799. Napoleon engaged in several successful military campaigns increasing France's wealth and position in Europe and his popularity. Throughout his career, he fought approximately sixty battles and only lost seven, most of those at the end of his career.

By this time, Napoleon and King George III of England had the greatest maritime war fleets in the world. As Napoleon conquered and annexed more and more of the European nations under the flag of France, he used his position to blockade supplies from Europe to the UK. Goods were still reaching the British Empire, however, mostly through Russia and parts of Spain that had yet to fall to the Emperor's insatiable acquisition of Europe.

America at this time maintained an isolationist policy, refusing to get involved despite the pressure of the French who had aided the young country in the revolution against what France saw as a mutual enemy (Great Britain) less than thirty years previously.

All this time, America had been trading goods with both sides of the conflict until President Jefferson declared an embargo against trading with either Kingdom or Empire. This policy soon proved to not only be ineffective but drastically backfired when neither England nor France much missed the American goods, and barely noticed the embargo. But American industry, dependent on exports, began to suffer.

The American embargo was seen by many to have crippled the American economy without making a single impact on the war in Europe. In 1808, the embargo was repealed.

Jefferson's idea to restrict trade with Europe was largely due to a desire to protect American ships and sailors. Plying the waters of two naval superpowers at war with each other was a risky proposition at best, and Great Britain had a long tradition of impressment.

During this time, it was within British law to sweep the streets of England and forcibly take fit men in order to press them into service on a naval vessel. This was called impressment. There were few professions who had a legal immunity to impressment, but even these were required to hold papers with them at all times. Unfortunately, the majority of men who were pressed into service were either drunk or severely beaten and pressed while unconscious. Presenting papers in such a condition posed something of a problem.

Seeking more experienced sailors, pressing men from commercial or fishing vessels became more common. British ships could be randomly boarded, her crew subject to being pressed into the Royal Navy. Foreign ships were officially exempt from boarding, however this was generally ignored - especially so with American ships.

Any American sailor that could not prove his citizenship was automatically assumed to be British and therefore subject to impressment. Some English sailors, who had left Great Britain to avoid the wars and the ever-present need for more sailors, joined American commercial ships and were re-impressed into the British Navy, often as traitors. Some estimates put pressed American sailors at about a thousand men every year.

In 1807, two British warships, the Halifax and the Malampus, were stationed off of Norfolk watching two storm-damaged French ships that had put in for repair. The pressed men on these British ships saw the American land within swimming distance. Three men, all Americans who had been pressed into service, and fourth British sailor similarly pressed, jumped overboard and took their chances.

British demands for the return of the deserters were ignored by the American government. The four men made their way to Portsmouth and signed up on the Chesapeake, bound for the Mediterranean. The HMS Leopard hailed the Chesapeake, demanding the return of the four men. When the commander of the Chesapeake refused, the Leopard fired seven shots into the unprepared frigate. The severely damaged American vessel had little choice but to allow the British man-o-war to board her and take the four men. The three Americans were imprisoned and the English deserter was hanged.

It was the American outrage at the Chesapeake affair that caused President Jefferson to create the embargo of 1807, and to call out and organize 100,000 militia in preparation for the war that was now all but inevitable.

British and French embargos heated up and both Kingdom and Empire decreed that any foreign vessel caught supplying or trading with the other side would be confiscated. In the meantime, impressment of American sailors continued and both Great Britain and France continued their respective embargos.

When an American sailor was "arrested" by the British ship Guerrière from an American merchant ship, the American warship President chased after the British ship, hoping to retrieve the man. In the nighttime fog, the President came across an unknown British ship. After a brief exchange, the President opened fire on the English ship, only later to realize it was the Little Belt and not the Guerrière.

The Little Belt was outgunned, 22 cannons to the President's 44. The Little Belt was decimated with the loss of nine crewmen, with 22 more injured. American popular opinion called this justice for the Chesapeake/ Leopard incident.

When Americans discovered that England had begun supplying Native Americans in Canada with weapons and a promise to restore all lands in what would later be considered the American Midwest to the natives, the tensions between America and England boiled over. Like Napoleon who had found himself battling on several fronts, America and England fell into the war Jefferson had been trying to avoid.

And so on June 18, 1812, the War they had been fighting for years officially began.

Chapter Two

From Tippecanoe to War Hawks

The rise of a dynamic Native American spiritual leader Tenskwatawa came as the result of several visions.

In 1805, while lighting his pipe, Tenskwatawa, a Shawnee who had very little going for him prior to this, and was known to be rather useless in hunting or battle, fell into a trance. Those that knew him attributed his condition to alcohol and thought that perhaps he had died. Instead he woke up and claimed to have had long conversations with The Master of Life, a deity who felt the Shawnee had forgotten their ways.

Tenskwatawa became known as a great medicine man, and was even considered a prophet – a title he would take for himself later on. He gathered followers who felt strongly that the white man was to blame for their condition and gave them a set of rules that had been given to him in his visions. He forbade his followers from using goods made by the whites. They could not trade or have any interaction with these "children of the Evil Spirit". He even led a purification movement to rid Native Americans of the evil influences of the whites and of Native American witches. Eventually, Tenskwatawa founded a community of followers at Greenville, Ohio.

Denounced by Territorial Governor William Henry Harrison as a fraud, Tenskwatawa predicted a solar eclipse in 1806. When the derided prediction came true, Harrison was publicly humiliated and Tenskwatawa was taken as a true prophet.

In 1808, Tenskwatawa's followers gathered in a semi-permanent settlement named after the leader – Prophetstown. Located at the juncture of the Tippecanoe and Wabash rivers, the settlement was also called Tippecanoe—a name a little more familiar to students of history.

Tenskwatawa wasn't the only charismatic leader in the family. Thousands of warriors were also gathering under the leadership of his brother, Tecumseh, an experienced warrior in his own right who had fought the white man's expansion into their territory at the Battle of Fallen Timbers. Notably, a young William Henry Harrison was also at that battle. Unlike other Native American leaders at the Battle of Fallen Timbers, Tecumseh refused to sign the treaty and began building a coalition of warriors to fend off westward expansion.

Tippecanoe, a large, organized pocket of the Native American confederacy, stood right in the way of westward expansion.

The stage was set. Unfortunately for Tecumseh, he was away recruiting more warriors when Governor Harrison arrived with 1,000 men. While initially Tenskwatawa seemed to want to talk, negotiations fell apart. While no one is quite sure how the battle began – whether it was under orders of the Prophet, or a result of panicked followers - the battle commenced on November 7, 1811. Though Tenskwatawa was a prophet and visionary, he was not a military leader. The settlement fell to Harrison's army, though it did sustain heavy losses in the process. The confederacy abandoned the site and Harrison's army burned the encampment to the ground.

American opinion placed blame for the Native American conflict on the British. General Andrew Jackson blamed the British for causing unrest among the natives. Tecumseh wasn't about to give up the fight; he realized he would need British support if he was to stop the white expansion. Tecumseh headed north and found British allies there in Ontario.

By this time the American people had had quite enough. An off-shoot of the Republican Party who called themselves the War Hawks came into being. Made up of several congressmen, including the likes of Henry Clay and John C. Calhoun, they wielded enough power to make things happen. They whipped the nation into a patriotic fervor against Britain. The fear of impressment and the constant harassment by Native Americans in the Northwest (bought and paid for by Great Britain) had taken its toll. And war, if done correctly, might win them Florida away from Spanish control.

The pressure was intense. On June 18, 1812, President Madison signed a declaration of war against Great Britain. America was still a young country, untested, and now at war with the greatest naval power in history.

Chapter Three

The War in the North

The first line of attack was Upper Canada, then a British colony. Lower Canada was protected by its very remoteness and a strong fortress in Quebec. The Maritime provinces of New Brunswick, Nova Scotia, and Prince Edward Island were protected by the British fleet, but Upper Canada was largely populated by Americans, and was only lightly defended.

Unfortunately, the American forces were unprepared. They outnumbered the British defenders, but the British commander, Major-General Sir Isaac Brock, had seen the inevitability of an American-English conflict and had spent the previous eight months preparing for battle. Of all the defenses he'd readied, perhaps the most important was making allies of the First Nations—the natives of Canada who numbered over 600 tribes.

Major-General Brock joined with Tecumseh and took a key American post at Michilimackinac Island in Lake Huron on July 17. The capture was quick and bloodless, and the emboldened British and Aboriginal forces pressed on into Detroit where Brock demanded the surrender from the American General William Hull.

Hull had spent the war thus far in writing threats, warning what would happen to the enemy if they should come. He should have been more careful with his more personal correspondence, as rather detailed information about troops and movements fell into enemy hands. By the time the British were ready to engage in battle, they knew everything they needed to know to make the entire campaign a success.

By this time, Hull had been vacillating too long. The more indecisive he got, the more he lost his nerve. When Brock demanded surrender, he quickly gave up the fort. Later he tried to save face by claiming he'd done it for the civilians, but his military career was pretty much over from this point on. When he was returned to the Americans in a prisoner exchange in 1814, he would face court-martial and the threat of execution.

On August 16, British and Aboriginal forces occupied the city. Brock's forces had full control of Michigan territory, all the way to the head of the Mississippi river.

Jefferson's boast that victory in Canada was "a matter of marching" came home to haunt Washington. Less than one month after losing the army and Detroit, the American forces lost another campaign at Queenston Heights.

On October 13, 1812, the American militia refused to enter Canada due in part to the British artillery, but also in part to their lack of training and experience. Despite the initial American advantage in numbers, the British forces were reinforced; America lost the first major battle involving actual military engagement in the War of 1812.

Tecumseh survived the battle, but Major-General Sir Isaac Brock was killed. The command of the British forces fell to Major-General Roger Hale Sheaffe. The British reinforcement took the American positions, causing the

American regulars, now unsupported by the militia, to surrender.

Queenston Heights was one of a four-pronged attack against Canada proposed by American forces. The other "prongs" had been equally disastrous. The first was to be led by General Hull. With his surrender at Detroit, this entire mission failed. The next was to be led by General Henry Dearborn, who remained inactive in New York. The last was under Major-General Van Rensselaer who had insufficient men and supplies to attack. Even if he had, Van Rensselaer was not a warrior, and had never commanded men in battle. He was, on the other hand, a candidate for governor of New York.

In 1813, things started getting interesting.

British strategy turned to one of defense, preferring to allow the Americans to attack and make mistakes. An attempt by the Americans to seize Kingston and thereby cut Canada in half turned into an attack on a lesser prize, the city of York (Toronto). American forces took over the city, burned public buildings, and appropriated supplies bound for British troops in the Great Lakes. But the goal of seizing the nearly finished British warship at York was frustrated when British forces burned the hull. Neither side controlled Lake Ontario from that point on until the end of the war.

On May 27, 1813, American forces captured Fort George at the mouth of the Niagara River. On the night of June 5th, British General John Vincent, who was retreating with his army from Fort George, turned on the American pursuers at Stoney Creek. In the American defeat that followed, two generals were captured and made prisoners by the British. Three weeks later at Beaver Dams, the American forces faced yet another defeat when 600 men were captured by the First Nations.

On October 5th, Major-General Henry Proctor led the occupiers of Detroit until the American navy gained control of Lake Erie and cut off Detroit's supplies. The occupiers were then forced to withdraw up the river Thames to Moraviantown, where the First Nations under the command of Tecumseh were forced to follow. American troops under the command of William Henry Harrison drove off the British and defeated the First Nations. Tecumseh was killed in this battle.

On December 10th, worn out by loss, illness, and desertion, American forces quit Fort George and left Canada. Upon leaving, American forces burned the city of Newark (Nigeria-on-the-Lake), setting a precedent of retaliation that would continue until Washington DC itself was burned by the British at the end of the war.

In April of 1814, Napoleon abdicated the throne of France, ending the British involvement in the wars in Europe. England now was able to focus more troops and energies into the American war.

Lieutenant General Sir George Prévost, the Commander-In-Chief in Canada and the Canadian Governor, received orders authorizing him to launch attacks into America.

Prévost launched a major offensive to Lake Champlain up the Richelieu River, as it was the only way from the lake to the ocean. Prévost advanced down the western

New York side of the lake and on to Plattsburgh. 8,000 troops were put under the command of the Lieutenant Governor of Lower Canada, Major-General Sir Francis Rottenburg. The British commanders under Prévost had had more battle experience and Prévost was not a popular commander, having a reputation for caution.

Plattsburgh was defended by 5,500 American troops under the command of Major-General George Izard, but he received orders to march to Sackett's Harbor, leaving Plattsburgh defended by 1,500 men under the command of Brigadier General Alexander Macomb. These were the troops unable to make the march to Sackett's Harbor, either through infirmity or due to poor training. Macomb called on the New York militia and pleaded for reinforcements from Vermont. Eventually his numbers were reinforced by 2,000 militia who had no training and were not a cohesive fighting force.

Though Macomb attempted to strengthen the fort's defenses, the citizens of Plattsburgh had so little faith in the defenders that they fled the town. Plattsburgh was inhabited solely by the American army and militia.

Lieutenant Thomas Macdonough commanded the American naval forces and constructed several gun boats. He and Commodore Isaac Chauncey contended for a limited number of experienced sailors and supplies. Macdonough was limited in his construction ability until his envoy argued his case in Washington.

Washington allowed two more ships, adding 60 more guns on the water and giving American forces superiority.

Prévost, for his part added another 36-gun frigate days before the battle.

On August 31st, Prévost set south. Macomb sent 1200 men and two 6-pound guns to fight a delaying action at Chazy, New York. The Americans began a slow fighting retreat, burning bridges, setting up road blocks, and harassing the enemy—ultimately delaying Prévost's arrival in Plattsburgh until September 6th.

Prévost ordered Major General Robinson to cross the Saranac, but could not supply Robinson with any intelligence on American placement or numbers. Tentative attempts to cross the bridges were repulsed by the defenders. Dropping plans to cross the river, Prévost began building batteries, and American forces responded by firing heated cannonballs and setting fire to the buildings the British were using as cover. This forced Prévost's troops to withdraw further.

Prévost had planned on attacking over a ford three miles above Macomb's defenses once Captain George Downie arrived with the new 36-gun frigate. Macomb knew that the British had better range and withdrew to Plattsburgh Bay, forcing the British to fight at close range. When Downie arrived on September 9th, the winds were unfavorable and he was not able to move into position. But the wind shifted the night of the 10th, and in the predawn, the British sailed into Plattsburgh, Captain Downie reconnoitering from a rowboat.

Downie maneuvered the Confidence into position, next to Macomb's flagship The Saratoga. Reaching his goal, he methodically secured his ship, preparing her for battle even as she took hit after hit from the American warship.

The Confidence finally responded with a single broadside that either killed or wounded a fifth of Saratoga's crew. Macomb was unhurt, but minutes later, Downie was killed when one of Confidence's cannons was hit and flew free of its carriage, crushing him.

The English ship Chubb was set adrift and the crew surrendered. Her sister ship Finch drifted aground, though barely hit at all. Macomb ordered Saratoga's anchor cut and the kedge anchors hauled in, spinning the ship around to bring her unused batteries to bear on the Confidence. The English ship was unable to meet this new threat and the British invasion force was forced to surrender.

Prévost, waiting on land with his troops, received the notice that the Confidence was destroyed. He had no choice but to retreat, as his supplies were cut off without naval support.

The news of the loss of the Battle of Plattsburgh reached Ghent, where the British confidence in the American capitulation of their demands was thoroughly shaken.

Chapter Four

The Battles of the Middle United States: Iowa and Lake Erie

Meanwhile, things were happening in other parts of the fledgling nation.

The Native American tribes dispersed at Prophetstown in 1811 did not disappear. While Tecumseh led many north to join British forces, many headed west to what was then the remote frontier of Iowa.

Built in 1807 as a bulwark to enforce the treaty with the Sauk Natives, Fort Belle View was small and unassuming. Unfortunately, it was under attack almost from the very beginning. In his memoirs, Black Hawk, a war leader of the Sauk, claimed that they were told the soldiers where building a home for a trader that was "coming to there to live and sell us goods very cheap." It quickly became apparent, however, that the fort was being built for other reasons, and indeed interrupted trade routes with the Natives.

Reinforced and enlarged, Fort Belle View was renamed to Fort Madison in honor of the fourth American President. This would prove to be serendipitous to the approaching war of 1812. In March of that year, before war was even formally declared with the British, a coordinated attack from the Sauk and affiliated tribes pummeled the fort. This was followed by another attack in September, when the British-backed-and-supplied Natives nearly overran the fort. Fort Madison was ultimately saved by cannon fire, which decimated the Sauk position. Black Hawk recounts personally shooting the flag off the pole during the battle. Sometime close on the heels of that battle, the fort was abandoned and burned, the soldiers retreating in the night to the Mississippi River.

One month later, in October of that year, Oliver Hazzard Perry was commissioned to the rank of Master Commandant. Transferred to Lake Erie in February of 1813, Perry began building ships in a race against the British Commander Robert Barclay. Over the next few months, Perry was able to build two brigs and seven smaller vessels.

Barclay deployed several ships to blockade Perry in May of 1813, but ultimately had to pull out to resupply his own vessels a few months later in July. Taking advantage of the sudden opportunity, Perry removed his fleet from the harbor while Barclay's back was turned. Barclay returned four days later to find Perry gone. Nothing was left but to take control of the lake and wait for his newest ship, The Detroit (named after the city recently fallen to British hands) to be completed. Barclay effectively was able to cut off all supplies through control of Lake Erie. It looked like a clear victory in terms of territory won and controlled. Then in September, Perry's fleet engaged.

Perry took command of The Lawrence while his second-in-command took the other brig, The Niagara, into the fight. It's not known why The Niagara slowed during the attack, but The Lawrence was left to face the enemy alone while waiting for the rest of the American fleet to catch up. The Lawrence was pounded by the six British ships, which included the HMS Little Belt.

The Lawrence was heavily damaged in the fight, taking 80% casualties. Perry ordered a boat lowered and transferred his flag to The Niagara. Making up lost speed, Perry attacked the British ships who attempted to turn to face this new threat, but the two largest of the English ships became entangled in each other in the close quarters. Perry pounded them as they flailed, struggling mightily to separate. The Niagara, backed by the arriving remainder of American gunboats, forced the British fleet into surrender. America had control once again of Lake Erie. Reporting to General William Henry Harrison, Perry famously wrote, "We have met the enemy and he is ours."

Chapter Five

The Lord Willing and the Creek Don't Rise

On August 30, 1813, the war reached the southern United States. In Alabama, aboriginal Americans stormed Fort Mims. The Americans had not been at war with the Creek tribe, but a faction known as "Red Sticks" because of their red-painted war clubs opposed the white expansion. They and were supplied not by Britain in this case, but by Spain through their governor in Florida.

The Red Sticks were one-time followers of Tenskwatawa and Tecumseh, who had fled south following the massacre at Tippecanoe. They followed a new prophet, Paddy Walsh, and the accomplished leader, William Weatherford, who would continue to cause damage throughout the South for the remainder of the year.

Keeping in mind that this was the south and Fort Mims was not much more than a stockade around a plantation, not everyone at the fort were on the side of the white man. Several black slaves, freed in the attack, joined the Red Sticks.

The end result wasn't pretty. Somewhere in the neighborhood of 250 people were killed – this number including a large number of women and children. Some say this number is conservative in estimate. It can also be pointed out that the Red Sticks took heavy losses as well, but they clearly won the day, giving this battle its name: The Fort Mims Massacre.

The defeat and reported mass killings of settlers, including women and children, drove nearby settlers to flee to Mobile, which was unprepared to accept a large inrush of refugees.

Popular opinion of the Native attack demanded retribution, and more importantly, protection from further attacks. However, America had its forces to the north fighting the British and had little enough to spare in the south. The states of Tennessee, Georgia, and the Mississippi Territory joined their militia to combat the threat of the Red Sticks. As the three militia became a cohesive unit, they found a new leader: Andrew Jackson. Jackson's militia of 2,600 soldiers, joined by 500 Cherokee allies, finally defeated the Red Sticks in March of 1814.

Andrew Jackson was a rising star on the political scene. Not privileged at birth, he'd worked hard to make something of himself. By this point in his career he'd found wealth and power as a lawyer and young politician. Here he had proven himself a military leader, and cemented for himself a reputation that would lead him to the presidency of the United States in 1828.

In this battle though, he had his hands full. His own troops weren't interested in fighting, and more than once he had to act to keep the men from deserting. The story of shooting a would-be deserter to make an example of him would follow him into the race for president. On the other hand, it characterized Jackson as decisive and strong, given to action.

That desire for action would lead him to Tehopeka and what became known as the Battle of Horseshoe Bend. On March 27, 1814, with 3,200 men that included American forces, Cherokee, and Lower Creek tribes, Andrew Jackson surrounded the Red Sticks stronghold at Tehopeka. Two hours of cannon fire, followed by a bayonet charge and hand to hand combat wasn't enough to take down the enemy; the Red Sticks refused to surrender. In a fight that lasted five hours, of the 1,000 Red Sticks who defended Tehopeka, 800 were killed. Jackson's casualties were less than 50.

In the wake of the battle, one of the Red Sticks leaders Chief Menawa led 200 survivors south to Florida and Spanish protection.

Jackson's victory culminated with the Treaty of Fort Jackson on August 9, 1814. 23 million acres of land were ceded from the natives to the white government, comprising half of current central Alabama and much of Georgia. This land was not all taken from the Red Sticks, or indeed from the Creek. Much of the land Jackson claimed for America was also taken from the Cherokee, who had been his allies in the fight, and from the Lower Creek who had remained neutral through the battle; the Lower Creek had in fact pressed to adopt the ways of the white man and live in peace.

Jackson was promoted to Major-General for his service in the battle.

Chapter Six

The Patriot's War

While the battles against the Red Sticks might not seem to be part of the War of 1812, they were for two reasons. First, Tippecanoe had grown out of the native uprisings funded by Great Britain. Secondly, this led to what can be termed the Other War of 1812, The Patriot's War, which had the goal of taking East Florida from Spain – a long-held ambition of the War Hawks.

If France fought on two fronts, America began the War of 1812 already engaged in conflict on her shores. Spain had built several fortresses along the Florida coast. Mostly not colonized but for some Spanish holdings, Americans had been emigrating to the peninsula since 1790. These settlers were collectively called "Patriots" and were by and large eager to annex the territory to the fledgling country.

Nominally to "protect" the Americans living in Florida, President Madison and Secretary of State James Monroe appointed General George Mathews to lead a contingent to prevent the British from securing a stronghold in the south. Congress passed a "secret" act of acquisition for Florida.

By the March of 1812, the Patriots joined with the American Navy seized Fernandina and Amelia Island. Nine gunboats lined the harbor and demanded the surrender of Fort San Carlos. Acknowledging the superior force, Don Justo Lopez, commander of the Spanish forces, surrendered the fort and island to the Patriots, who raised their own flag. The following day, a regular detachment of 250 troops under the command of Mathews were dispatched to the fort. They struck the Patriot's flag and raised the American stars and stripes.

Fearing the alienation of the Patriots and open declaration of war with Spain as well as with Britain, Congress publically condemned the act. Secretary of State Monroe was forced to relieve Mathews of his commission. The American troops left the fort, striking the flag and departed for Georgia, ceding control back to the Spanish after nearly a year since its capture.

President Monroe quietly appointed the Governor of Georgia David Brydie Mitchell to "oversee" events in Florida. By June of 1812, America was officially at war with Great Britain, and Great Britain was at war with France. One of Britain's staunchest allies was Spain, who now had a stronghold in American lands. Retaking Florida soon became a national issue.

Native Americans from the area known as the Seminoles and many warriors from Prophetstown joined with the Spanish, realizing the fears of the Patriots. The Spanish and their Native allies began raiding Patriot settlements and those of Patriot sympathizers.

Georgian Daniel Newnan commanded a unit of volunteers and marched into Florida to do battle with the Seminoles and their leader, King Payne. Newnan was shot with three musketballs and had to be evacuated to his plantation, but recovered miraculously fast. The largely successful actions of his men and their daring escape became a rally point for the American people around the annexation of Florida. This would be an issue not resolved until 1819.

In the meantime, things were getting interesting up north....

Chapter Seven

Washington in Flames

Things didn't look good for the Americans. In Canada there had been some initial success with the capture of Fort Erie at Niagara. Led by Major General Jacob Brown, the goal became the invasion of Upper Canada. On July 25th the stage was set for the bloodiest battle in the War of 1812.

The fight began in the evening – around 7 PM. The fighting quickly devolved into hand-to-hand combat, so close that musket fire went past the enemy. In the failing light, the scene was chaotic, and by morning the sight unimaginable. Dead and dying littered the field. Each side suffered casualties of nearly a thousand men – either dead, dying, or missing. The Americans hightailed it for Fort Erie, but even that stronghold wouldn't last. They wound up blowing up the fort and retreating back across the Niagara into New York State.

The British were now ready to invade.

In August of 1814, Vice Admiral Alexander Cochrane brought his fleet into Chesapeake Bay. The Americans recognized almost immediately that the target was their own capital – Washington D.C. The city became a ghost town, while the American force assembled at Bladensburg, MD. Sadly the troops they had were mostly untrained militia. President Madison himself was at the battle, and retreated along with the troops. The road was now open to Washington.

The president's wife, First Lady Dolley Madison, famously had stayed behind. While her contemporaries fled the city, she was busy packing trunks full of important documents and rescuing the famous portrait of George Washington from the wall of the White House (little did she know that it was only a copy; the original was safely elsewhere). It is said that they left the White House so quickly that dinner was still on the table and still warm when the enemy arrived. Whether this is urban legend or truth, no one knows. But either way things happened quickly – and the White House was soon occupied by British who wasted no time in looting the place, right down to stealing the president's love letters penned by his wife.

While General Ross had led the troops into Washington, it was Admiral Cockburn who ordered it burned. Ross had originally wanted to ransom the city back to the Americans, but there just wasn't anyone around to negotiate with and Cockburn got his way. Several sites of great importance were burned immediately – the Navy Yard, the War Office, and the Treasury Building. The Capitol and White House were thoroughly ransacked and also set ablaze. Rain storms put out several of the fires, so they were ordered re-kindled the next day just to make sure the deed was done properly.

Why so brutal? Let's remember that the precedent for destroying cities and settlements had started with the Americans back in Tippecanoe. Destruction had followed almost every battle—inflicted by both sides. By this point in the war, Vice-Admiral Cochrane had expressed that the

Americans "needed a good drubbing." As evidenced here, there were plenty in the British forces who shared that sentiment and who were only too willing to oblige.

It is said that you could see the glow on the horizon of the burning city as far away as Baltimore. This was, perhaps, a sign of things to come.

Chapter Eight

The Battle for Baltimore

Outside of Baltimore, Maryland, a star-shaped fortress was built in 1798 on the remains of an older fort, Fort Whetstone. Fort McHenry, as it came to be known, was designed to protect the ever-increasingly important Port of Baltimore from all future enemies. Surrounded by a dry moat, Fort McHenry boasted 18, 24, and 32-pound cannons. The design and defenses were severely tested on September 13, 1814.

Vice Admiral Alexander Cochrane had recently come from a victory in New York and from delivering troops to Washington D.C. He had pressed to take Rhode Island, but his superiors wanted a larger prize, and so Cochrane set sail for Baltimore. Wanting to minimize casualties and take the fort as a usable defense, Cochrane set about bombarding the Fort McHenry with bombs and rockets. Cochrane fought his junior officers, who insisted he take his frigates and attack at close range, as the admiral preferred a less aggressive attack.

While the bombardment continued, Cochrane, Rear Admiral George Cockburn, and Major General Robert Ross welcomed on board two Americans to the Tonnant. The Americans were there to negotiate the release of prisoners, one of them being Dr. William Beanes, who had jailed marauding British troops and had himself been arrested by the British.

After having arrived on the command ship of the blockade in Baltimore, Beanes and the two negotiators, John Skinner and Francis Scott Key, had learned too much of the enemy's strengths and positions and so were not allowed to leave. The negotiators were themselves taken prisoner.

The bombardment of Fort Henry lasted for 25 hours. The accuracy at the range of the attacker's positions was low, but the Americans, having been warned of the British intent to take Baltimore, had sunk 22 ships at the harbor. Between the sunken ships and the cannon fire, the British were unable to take Baltimore.

Due to the extreme range, the rockets and bombs were relatively ineffective. Americans suffered four dead, one of which was a civilian. The British had no losses and one wounded crewman. Fort McHenry took no appreciable damage and only one British ship was struck by an American cannon.

At dawn, the three American prisoners on the Tonnant watched as British rockets streaked through the rising sun and saw that the over-sized American flag still snapped and flowed in the wind. It is said that Key was later inspired by that sight to write a poem called Defence of Fort Henry. Soon thereafter, Key took his poem to a music publisher and set it to a popular tune called "To Anacreaon in Heaven" and renamed it "The Star Spangled Banner". It was more than a century later that "The Star Spangled Banner" was adopted as the American anthem.

Meanwhile, the land attack coordinated by General Ross of the British forces failed miserably.

The burning of Washington had been designed to make the Americans cower before the might of the British forces. Instead, the Americans had become outraged. In Baltimore, far from fleeing the city as had happened in Washington, the people had stayed to fight - and fight they did. Every person who was able-bodied, be they men, women, or even children, had dug trenches and constructed defensive lines. Volunteers had appeared from every corner of the countryside, swelling the militia to 12,000.

As the British lines advanced, the militia sent out 3,000 men to greet them. The Americans fought creatively, using sniper fire to harass the British troops. Ross himself was killed by a sniper's bullet, and the foreign invasion soon fell apart. More than 300 died on the British side, less than half that on the American. The city was considered too costly to take; retreat was called and the entire idea abandoned.

Baltimore was safe. The battle by land and by sea had lasted only 25 hours.

Chapter Nine

The Battle of New Orleans

From Baltimore, Cochrane turned his attention south. He wasn't the only one.

In September of 1814, Captain William Percy led his ships against Fort Bowyer in anticipation of an assault on Mobile, Alabama. Percy took 60 redcoats and an artillery piece, anticipating that Fort Bowyer would be an easy target. Fort Bowyer was little more than a hastily constructed stockade, with earthen and wooden walls.

Percy took The HMS Hermes, HMS Sophie, HMS Carron and HMS Childers. Between his vessels, Percy had 78 guns, more than a match for what he supposed was a platform for six to 14 small-caliber weapons.

The HMS Hermes took the point in the battle, and was soon joined by the HMS Sophie. However, the rest of his ships were unable to get into a position to engage the fort. After two hours, the HMS Hermes floundered and beached. The HMS Sophie took her crew and Percy ordered the HMS Hermes burned. The ship later exploded when the fire hit her powder magazines. The remaining ships anchored for the night a mile and a half away from the fort.

In the morning, Percy left the engagement. The British had lost 34 and had 35 wounded (4 men with mortal wounds), and the American defenders had lost four men and another five wounded. As the fort remained undefeated, however; the British plans to take Mobile were scrapped. Instead, Cochrane set sail for New Orleans. He would arrive there in December of 1814.

By the start of 1814, the landscape had shifted dramatically. England and France had ended their war and England was free to turn her full might against American shores. Washington had been burned by advancing British forces who were in turn stopped a Baltimore.

Andrew Jackson, now Major-General Jackson due to the success at the Creek wars, learned of a rumored invasion at either Mobile or New Orleans. Without waiting for orders, he mustered his troops and set off for Florida, entering Spanish-controlled areas to stem off invasions from Britain and to quell possible activity of the Seminoles. Jackson's military force consisted of regular troops, militia volunteers from three states and the Mississippi territory, freed blacks, Creoles, Native Americans, and even a band of pirates (more about them later).

Jackson's forces, though passionate, were outnumbered and inexperienced - and they were facing the deadliest military force on the planet.

On December 14th, Britain invaded Louisiana with little resistance from Jackson's hodge-podge army. For the next two weeks, the two forces stalemated while British forces attempted to find a way through the American defenses. Finding no easy way through Jackson's force, British troops conducted a full-scale attack on January 8th, 1815. The world was shocked when the disorganized and motley American army handed the British a crushing defeat, forcing them to withdraw from Louisiana.

The Battle of New Orleans was a decisive victory for Andrew Jackson. Sadly it came too late. Two weeks previous to what is arguably the greatest and bloodiest battle of the war, American and British envoys had signed a treaty at Ghent in Belgium. The distance between Belgium and Florida meant that neither American nor British forces received word of the treaty until after the battle was fought and won.

Yet even this would not be the last battle of the War of 1812. On February 11, 1815, the British returned to Fort Bowyer, this time with 3,000 troops, up against only a few hundred Americans inside the fort. The British forces were fresh from New Orleans, and had planned on taking Bowyer, so they could revert to the plan to take Mobile and return to New Orleans later. Cut off entirely by 38 ships, with no reinforcements in sight, fort commander William Lawrence surrendered, fearing the casualties would be too high.

While this was truly the last battle in the war, it was overshadowed by the much bigger (and bloodier) Battle for New Orleans. And since history books are always written by the winners, this conflict was quite "forgotten," especially as it ended the war on such a poor note for the Americans.

About this time, word filtered through to the troops about the Treaty of Ghent. So plans to attack Mobile were forgotten, and finally, in action as well as on paper, the war could finally end.

Chapter Ten

A Bit About Pirates

At the beginning of the war, the American fleet was no match for the British navy, who had established a global rule over the world's oceans. To fill the demand for more ships quickly, letters of Marque were issued to private vessels offering safe shelter for pirates that harassed enemy ships and left American vessels undisturbed.

One of the more famous of these privateers was Jean Lafitte, who had been harassing the Gulf Coast for many years before the outset of war. Based on the small island of Barataria, off the coast of Louisiana, Jean Laffite and his brother Pierre began his outlaw career by smuggling in goods from ships that had traded with foreign governments in violation of Jefferson's embargo of 1807.

Pierre was quieter than his flamboyant brother and remained on the island, seeing to the business of smuggled and stolen goods, while Jean moved the goods in through the Louisiana swamps, taking up to a full week to go what was a relatively short distance.

In October of 1812, the brothers purchased a schooner and hired Captain Trey Cook to command her. As the ship had no registration and indeed did not even have a name, Cook was considered to be a pirate and the schooner to be a pirate vessel.

In January of 1814, Captain Cook claimed his first prize: a Spanish brig carrying 77 slaves. Selling the stolen goods, as well as the slaves, generated $18,000 for the brothers. The brig was pressed into service as the second of their two ships. This ship was recommissioned as The Dora, and was quickly able to prove her worth when she captured another Spanish ship, this time a schooner, loaded down with over $9,000 in goods. As the schooner was not a useful pirate vessel, it was returned to its former captain.

Soon word of the brothers spread around the coast. They treated their prisoners fairly and with decency; more often than not, they would release captured enemies and return them to their ships. This reputation helped in the long run, as crews found it safer and easier to capitulate and surrender without battle.

The brothers soon added another ship, La Diliget, and outfitted it with 12 cannons. When they acquired another vessel they renamed Petite Milan, they stripped out their original ship and set her cannons on Milan.

For several months, the three ships held a veneer of respectability, bringing in legal cargo to New Orleans. With scant attention from authorities as to what they brought out of Louisiana, their smuggling operation flourished.

In June of 1812, war was declared between America and Great Britain. The American government issued six letters of marque to residents of Barataria. These letters authorized the pirates to capture ships and goods of British vessels which were then submitted to American authorities, but ships and goods taken from other countries were sold through the Laffite brother's operations. However, the Laffites were smugglers, not pirates, and thus did not have a letter of marque. Their enterprises however were costing Americans a small fortune due in part to the embargo, but also in part to Laffite's connections.

In November, the US District Attorney John R. Grimes charged Laffite with a "violation of the revenue tax" and the brothers were arrested along with 25 others. All of the arrested men posted bail and disappeared.

Still under indictment, Jean Laffite registered as Captain of Le Brig Goelette la Dilligente for a fictitious trip to New York. This registration was simply a ruse to establish Laffite as a "privateering captain". The ruse worked to an extent, as Laffite received a letter of Marque from Cartagena, but violated the terms of the letter by never bringing captured goods there but instead filtering everything through Barataria.

The Governor of Louisiana was so angered by Laffite that he offered a $500 reward for his capture. Within two days of the proclamation, handbills appeared all over New Orleans offering a $500 reward for the Governor, offered by Laffite. Pierre, however, was tried and convicted for conspiracy in his older brother's crimes.

In September 1814, the HMS Sophie, soon to join the attack on Fort Bowyer, fired upon Laffite. Laffite ground his ship in water too shallow for the large English ship to follow; Captain Nicholas Lockyer, captain of the HMS Sophie, and Captain John McWilliam, Captain of the Royal Marine Infantry, rowed out to meet with Laffite.

McWilliam had two letters for Laffite: one under the seal of King George, offering Laffite and his men British citizenship and lands if they aided the king in the fight against the Americans, and the other from McWilliam's supervisor Lt Colonel Edward Nicolls, urging Laffite to accept the king's offer.

Laffite believed that America would win, though the odds were stacked against the fledgling country. More to the point, he also understood that evading American revenuers would be much easier than avoiding British revenuers. Laffite had also gotten word that American forces were planning on storming Barataria, as they feared the pirates would join their enemies.

Wanting to prove to the American government that they had nothing to fear from him, Laffite sent copies of both letters to Jean Blanque, a member of the state legislature. Laffite committed himself and his men to the defense of New Orleans, reminded Blanque that his little brother Pierre was still in prison, and that he was deserving of an early release. Within two days, Pierre made a miraculous "escape" from prison. Jean Laffite joined the war.

On September 13, American Commodore Daniel Patterson in the USS Carolina, accompanied by six gunboats, attacked Barataria. The pirates mustered ten armed vessels but in a few hours abandoned their ships and fled, burning several. Patterson's men met no further resistance and captured 80 men. Laffite escaped capture again.

Appeals for clemency were sent to Andrew Jackson. The general refused, saying that Laffite could not be trusted, as he was a pirate after all.

When Jackson arrived in New Orleans on December 1st, he found the city unprepared and vulnerable. The city had two manned ships, and even though they held possession of the eight ships taken from Laffite, there were not enough experienced sailors to crew them. Laffite's men, resentful of the raid on their homes, refused to crew their former ships.

Jackson met with Laffite, who agreed to defend New Orleans on the condition of pardons for all the former crews who volunteered to fight for the city. Jackson agreed.

On December 23rd, British ships reached the Mississippi river. American ships were badly outnumbered and Laffite suggested to Jackson that their defensive line be extended to a nearby swamp.

Five days later, British ships opened fire and were repulsed by two of Laffite's former lieutenants. Laffite's men proved more capable than the British gunners. Laffite and the pirates of Barataria were granted clemency. Jean and Pierre received high praise from Jackson who said of them they "exhibited the same courage and fidelity."

Chapter Eleven

The Treaty of Ghent

The Treaty of Ghent effectively ended the War of 1812.

On Christmas Eve 1814, representatives from America and England signed a treaty in Ghent, Belgium. Though the official end of the war would not come until Congress agreed to the treaty in February, it was signed by England's Prince Regent. The news took over a month to reach Florida and Louisiana, however; in the meantime, the Battle of New Orleans and the Second Battle at Fort Bowyer raged between two nations technically at peace.

The treaty specified that all lands were to be restored to the state they were in before the hostilities began, thus negating all wins and losses in the war. In early negotiations, England pressed for a Native Barrier State in the American Northwest. This area would be set aside for Aboriginal Americans – so called "Indians" – and would be sponsored by England. This would also act as a buffer to curb white American expansion. This was the first of the treaty demands to be dropped.

President Monroe had rallied for England to cede Canada to American control. This too was dropped.

The only real provision made for the Native Americans was that all "possessions, rights and privileges that the natives may have enjoyed in 1811." This did make it into the final treaty, but was unenforceable; England soon lost interest in sponsoring the natives.

The first impasse came when England demanded that American naval forces stay off the Great Lakes, and that English ships have unrestricted trade access along the Mississippi River. American diplomats refused these terms.

In the backdrop of the disastrous Battle of Plattsburgh, the British public had had its belly full of war. Reputations had been destroyed, lives lost, commercial interests interrupted and destroyed, and all for no gain as neither side seemed to have done more than stalemate the other.

It was finally agreed that all lands would revert to who had owned them in 1811, and all prisoners to be exchanged. This also included a provision that all slaves be returned to their masters, something that could hardly have felt fair to the former slaves given places in the British military if they escaped to them, or to those slaves promised the ability to settle in Britain's colonies. Both of these things had been promised by Vice Admiral Alexander Cochrane (and carried out in terms of military service).

In effect, both sides agreed to revert back to their status as if the war had never happened.

With James Madison still acting as president, Congress unanimously ratified the Treaty of Ghent on February 16, 1815. The War was officially over.

Epilogue: And What Happened Next...

While Tenskwatawa lived through the war (the same couldn't be said for his brother, Tecumseh), he was never able to regain his position among the native tribes. He stayed in Canada until the mid-1820's, where he then spent his time in a project to bring all the Shawnee to Kansas, where he himself settled and later died in 1836.

William Henry Harrison found his way to American presidency post-war, running with John Tyler as his vice-president under the slogan "Tippecanoe and Tyler too," a reminder to the voters of his victory in that war. His success didn't last long though, as his term lasted only one month. He took office March 4, 1841, but stood out in rain to be sworn in. This resulted in his death from pneumonia on April 4, 1841, leaving Tyler to take up the mantle of the presidency.

In 1814, General William Hull faced court martial for his surrender of Detroit. Sentenced to die, James Madison stepped in and gave a stay of execution. Hull spent the rest of his life trying to clear his name – with little success.

Major-General Henry Proctor was court-marshalled for "deficiency in energy and judgement" at the Battle of the Thames, effectively ending his military career.

Lieutenant General Sir George Prévost was court-marshalled for his actions at Plattsburgh. He requested a military tribunal in which he was confident he would be vindicated, but died a month prior to the tribunal of dropsy, now called edema.

Brigadier General Alexander Macomb was eventually promoted to Commanding General of the Army, the highest position reporting only to the Secretary of War. Macomb received a Congressional Gold Medal for his actions at Plattsburgh.

When President Madison and his wife Dolley had to flee the White House ahead of British troops, they'd had to abandon the couple's personal belongings in favor of those government documents that Dolley chose to save instead. While the Madisons returned to Washington three days later, they never lived in the White House again. It was uninhabitable until James Monroe succeeded Madison as President in 1817.

Major-General Van Rensselaer served many years in Congress and had the dubious honor of casting the deciding vote that placed John Quincy Adams in the White House at the expense of Andrew Jackson. Rensselaer founded the Rensselaer Polytechnic Institute, "for the purpose of instructing persons, who may choose to apply themselves, in the application of science to the common purposes of life" in 1824.

Though technically Jackson's victory at New Orleans wasn't until after the treaty was signed, the battle was so one-sided and so unexpected that Jackson's fame rose along with his rank. He continued in the military, taking chief part in the Seminole War which ended in Spain ceding Florida to the United States. Jackson was later elected the American president and served from 1829-

1937 where he would continue to impact the shape of the country, especially in regards to how the Native Americans were handled.

Jean and Pierre Lafitte spied for the Spanish against the Mexicans at Galveston. Two weeks into his stay at the island, the Mexican revolutionary leaders left and Lafitte claimed Galveston as his own; with Spain's blessing, turned it into another smuggling port.

What is the impact of the War of 1812?

On the international stage, it was the peace that resulted between the United States and Great Britain. For two centuries, the countries have been able to act as friends and allies in the international arena. While the war has largely been forgotten in England, the impact is still felt in the relations between the countries, and hopefully will continue in years to come.

In Canada the War had an importance that makes it something every school child learns about, probably more so than their American counterparts to the south. To them the war was a fight for national survival against American oppression. Their suspicion of the American way of life then influenced their own government as they became an independent nation of their own. Would Canada have become part of the United States if the war had not happened, or had gone differently? It's hard to say, but one can argue reasonably well that Canada is the way it is today in part because of the War of 1812.

In America the impact was perhaps more profound than we know. As the War was winding down, delegates from five states had been meeting secretly with the goal of seceding from the United States. These were Massachusetts, Connecticut, New Hampshire, Rhode Island, and Vermont. On December 15, 1814 they met at the old Court House in Hartford, Connecticut to discuss the matter, little realizing that their entire basis for meeting – their opposition to the War of 1812 –was about to disappear. In little more than a week, the Treaty of Ghent would be signed, and the War would be over.

When news broke regarding the Treaty, the Hartford Convention no longer looked quite so appealing to the masses. With the War having been seen as a victory for democracy, the idea of succession seemed nothing short of treason. The movement died down quietly, and the country stayed intact – up until December 20, 1860, when the Southern states would secede from the Union.

But that's another story.

FREE STUFF!

As a way of saying thank you for reading my book, I'm offering you a free copy of below e-Book.
Enjoy!

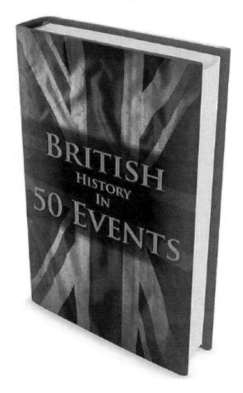

>> Click Here <<
>> To Get Your FREE eBook <<

1/4   102513   10.601

Made in the USA
Lexington, KY
01 July 2018